Revolution Handbook

August 22, 2011

by

William Bradford Cushman

Copyright © 2011 by William Bradford Cushman

ISBN-13: 978-1466234338

ISBN-10: 1466234334

Cover Credits

Liberty bell image from: McCabe, James D.; *The Pictorial History of the United States.* Philadelphia: The National Publishing Company, 1877.

Boston tea party image from: Butterworth, Hezekia.; *The Story of America.* New York: The Werner Company, 1898.

Many people today think that the Tea Act—which led to the Boston Tea Party—was simply an increase in the taxes on tea paid by American colonists. Instead, the purpose of the Tea Act was to give the East India Company full and unlimited access to the American tea trade and to exempt the company from having to pay taxes to Britain on tea exported to the American colonies. It even gave the company a tax refund on millions of pounds of tea that it was unable to sell and holding in inventory.

One purpose of the Tea Act was to increase the profitability of the East India Company to its stockholders (which included the king) and to help the company drive its colonial small-business competitors out of business. Because the company temporarily no longer had to pay high taxes to England and held a monopoly on the tea it sold in the American colonies, it was able to lower its tea prices to undercut those of the local importers and the mom-and-pop tea merchants and teahouses in every town in America.

This infuriated the independence-minded colonists, who were, by and large, unappreciative of their colonies' being used as a profit center for the multinational East India Company corporation. They resented their small businesses still having to pay the higher, pre-Tea Act taxes without having any say or vote in the matter (thus the cry of "no taxation without representation!").

Even in the official British version of the history, the 1773 Tea Act was a "legislative maneuver by the British ministry of Lord North to make English tea marketable in America," with a goal of helping the East India Company quickly "sell 17 million pounds of tea stored in England..."

From: "*Unequal Protection*": The Boston Tea Party Revealed by: Thom Hartmann, Berrett-Koehler Publishers[1]

We once had a revolution over the issue of government and the wealthy working together to take money from the rest of us, and now it's time for another.

---

[1]Excerpted at: http://www.truth-out.org/unequal-protection-boston-tea-party-revealed/1301986800

Dedication

This book is dedicated to all those brave individuals who yearn for justice and equality for all, and because of these noble feelings actively fight against tyranny wherever they may find it. These are the men and women who raise us all from the primordial swamp. I thank you all.

Contents

Chapter 1 — Democracy Is Stillborn In America

Democracy is not freedom.
Democracy is two wolves and a lamb
voting on what to eat for lunch.
Freedom comes from the recognition of
certain rights which may not be taken,
not even by a 99% vote.

Marvin Simkin, "Individual Rights", Los Angeles Times,
12 January 1992

THE FOUNDING FATHERS, being for the most part wealthy men, were very concerned that a true American democracy would expose them to a tyranny of the majority. This majority, they feared, would vote in their own self-interest to transfer private accumulations of great wealth to the nations treasury, and from there into the hands of the great unwashed masses of the common people. One method to prevent this feared redistribution of wealth was to limit voting to white male property owners. At the time the Constitution was written almost all significant wealth was in the form of real property, so limiting the vote to white male property owners was, in fact, an effective control on the feared tyranny of the masses. Limiting the vote to white male property owners also reflected an attitude prevalent among the Founding Fathers, that the wealthy had the *exclusive* right to rule. The "democracy" of the new United States was thus limited from its very beginning to those who have always been in actual control of the country: the wealthy elite.

History has since proven that limiting suffrage as a protective method was doomed to failure as over time the poor, women, and people of darker skin all fought for and won their suffrage. Limiting suffrage was not the only, or the most effective step taken to protect the wealthy, however. The wealthy of the time were exceedingly clever. A much more subtle means of retaining real control of the country in wealthy hands was carefully built into the Constitution in plain sight, without any public comment on the underlying intent. This deception was accomplished very simply, and its use reveals an extremely sophisticated understanding of human nature. That deception was simply this: it was decided by the country's Founding Fathers that our new country would not be a democracy at all, but a republic. There are many valid arguments for forming a republic instead of a democracy that have nothing to do with control by the wealthy, and these were discussed extensively in The Federalist Papers of the time. These arguments proved persuasive, and our new republic was formed with the clear approval of a deceived people. The issue completely overlooked in the public arguments presented, but which must have been of particular interest to the wealthy, was this: *a republic would greatly limit the number of individuals "representing" the people that would need to be convinced to leave great wealth intact.* Moreover, the probability that those elected representatives would be "cooperative" could be increased dramatically if those representatives were themselves wealthy, or if not already wealthy assisted and encouraged to become wealthy.

At the time of our new nation's infancy a welcoming warm fire, a few cigars, and diner with the families of the rich and powerful would have gone far to encourage "our" new representatives and senators, and even a President, to feel a part of the wealthy ruling class. The welcoming arms of the wealthy and powerful would serve to emotionally encourage joining this class in spirit, even if the new representatives were not already wealthy in fact. Wealth means power in all cases, and power is universally addictive. The converse is also true, the successful achievement of power will inevitably result in wealth. Unfortunately, the unmitigated grasping for either power or wealth will displace a very important concept from the enlightenment era: personal honor. Few people today recognize that honor is equal in value to life itself.[2] Honor is something we do for ourselves, because without honor and its attendant values we are nothing but silly mechanisms futilely plodding mechanically through a brief existence without meaning.

In our modern times the newly elected are either already wealthy, or will soon be wealthy. If the unheard of should occur and the people elect a "representative" that is not initially wealthy, this poor "representative" will be helpless against the wealthy majority. His minority status will serve to prevent any action that threatens the control held firmly in the hands of the wealthy. With control and the status quo thus maintained, time becomes available for a poor representative in congress to be co-

---

[2] "Give me Liberty, or give me Death!" Patrick Henry, 23 March, 1775

opted. This co-option is most easily done by providing the means by which the "people's" representative can *become* wealthy. A newly made wealthy "representative" thus joins the ranks of the wealthy elite, with the self-interest that entails. There are many ways in which a new representative can be made wealthy, but direct bribery is clearly the preferred means. Of course the term "bribery" is not used for reasons of political correctness, the more acceptable term: "campaign contribution" is used in its place.

Until the law was recently changed, congress had enjoyed the benefits of self serving laws enabling money collected for political campaigns, but never used, to pass directly to the representative or senator *as personal property* upon retirement.[3] These funds were, therefore, effectively legally laundered for the recipients upon retirement from public service. The incentive to make these funds as massive as possible was obvious. Now, after the stench of this practice afflicted noses nationwide and forced a change, the law requires that upon retirement unused funds not be used for "personal use." These funds may be used for anything else,[4] or simply held indefinitely. The definition of "personal use" is, of course, a massive loophole through which any politician with half a brain could drive an aircraft carrier. Rest assured that "campaign contributions" have not lost their ability to *persuade or induce.*

The results from a persistent program of facilitating the acquisition of wealth by "our representatives" are remarkable. Our history has proven that a senator who is himself a wealthy man will not quickly raise taxes on wealth if he can find any excuse to justify avoiding it.

---

[3]http://www.opensecrets.org/news/2008/02/retirement-funds.html

[4]http://www.opensecrets.org/news/2010/03/the-retirement-announcement-la.html

Nor will he pass any legislation that will encumber the "friends" he has cultivated among the wealthy that provide the money for his campaign expenses and other more direct avenues to wealth. Most importantly from the point of view of the wealthy, these co-opted "representatives" have proved themselves anxious to be of service to their masters, and the return on investment for those masters has been outstanding.

Our new "democracy" was thus doubly thwarted in fact from the very beginning of its existence; while at the same time giving the false public impression that it thrived. In hindsight, it now seems unlikely that the wealthy men who wrote the Constitution would have approved this potentially dangerous document had they not been comfortable with the built-in means of control it provided.

HAVE THE TWO methods used to maintain control by the wealthy elite been effective? The first method of restricted suffrage was a clear offense to the majority of the population, was recognized as such, and was bitterly fought and eventually overthrown, piece by piece. We now have fairly universal voter suffrage, at least in law, thus removing that direct Constitutional protection of the wealthy from the tyranny of the masses. The other, more subtle, means of simply subverting and assimilating our representatives, remains. This later method has worked extremely well — for the wealthy elite. Exactly how well is evident from the following study.

In 2005 Larry M. Bartels of the Department of Politics and Woodrow Wilson School of Public and International Affairs, Princeton University, published a very interesting study entitled: "*Economic Inequality and Political Representation*"[5] in which he directly addressed the issue of

---

[5]http://www.scribd.com/doc/36931202/Larry-Bartels-

representation in the Senate as a function of the economic status of the citizens presumed to be represented. The results demonstrated what most people who watch United States politics would guess: *if you are of low economic status neither a Democrat or a Republican will represent your interests — at all*. The situation improves as your economic status improves, until citizens with obscenely high incomes enjoy very good representation indeed. Professor Bartels comments that: *"These disparities [in representation] are especially troubling because they suggest the potential for a debilitating feedback cycle linking the economic and political realms:* **increasing economic inequality may produce increasing inequality in political responsiveness, which in turn produces public policies increasingly detrimental to the interests of poor citizens, which in turn produces even greater economic inequality, and so on.**[6] (Emphasis added.)"

Dr. Bartels concern has been completely realized. The United States government now works *exclusively* for the wealthy, and our politicians have no real choice in this matter, given how the current system has evolved. No national politician has any chance of election whatsoever without the funding and the access to public media received from wealthy sources. Funding and access to the media are the carrot, but also the stick. Should any politician attempt any stance that favors the general population at the expense of the wealthy, it is clear to all that there will be no future funding or access for that politician, and that politician will usually be publicly crucified by this same media to make certain his removal. No lie is

---

Economic-Inequality-and-Political-Representation
  [6]*ibid*, page 31

too egregious for our modern mass media. Anyone can be destroyed in this manner.

All of our politicians will swear defensively that the money they receive from their wealthy patrons has no influence over their decisions, but the data that Dr. Bartels has collected clearly make a lie of this contention. Simple logic also makes a lie of this contention: our politicians would not have their plush and lucrative jobs without this money. The money functions, therefore, as a bribe, as completely demonstrated by it's effect. It is given *"to persuade or induce,"* and that is the simple definition of a bribe. There is, however, another closely related definition of interest in this regard. A definition that defines a relationship with an extremely nasty history; because it defines a political system that is dependent upon the bundling[7] of the two most powerful segments of any political entity; **government** *and* **business leadership**.

> **Fascism** n. *A philosophy or system of government that advocates or exercises a dictatorship of the extreme right,* **typically through the merging of state and business leadership**, *together with an ideology of belligerent nationalism.*[8]

So, where are we now? The practice of co-opting the people's representatives has always been a serious problem in the United States, but was ameliorated somewhat when the concept of honor was still given lip service by the wealthy elite. During the early years of our new nation elections were still relatively transparent as well, so

---

[7]**Fascis** /ˈfæsiːz/ Is the Latin word meaning "bundle."

[8]*New College Edition of the American Heritage Dictionary of the English Language*, Copyright 1969, Houghton Mifflen

the public did have access to the electoral option to punish egregious political behavior by their representatives. Now, however, the concept of honor has been relegated to the realm of the "quaint," along with our Constitution, and elections are completely opaque since the advent of electronic voting.

The wealthy have also used their mass media to effectively change the public perception of what is "proper" behavior. This process has been exacerbated and exploited by dishonorable people such as Milton Freidman, who provided comforting palliatives for the wealthy, publicly espoused. Palliatives like "Greed is good." This process of currying favor from the wealthy by supplying "moral cover" has moved the moral goalposts far away from what would once be accepted as minimal moral political behavior. It is an integral part of a process that has devolved our public moral stance to the point where an opinion that "greed is good" is now actually viewed as valid in the halls of power.

The concept that greed is good is an opinion that would appall most of the Founding Fathers of this nation. But, it is a concept that is convenient to justify the present extreme income inequality between rich and poor, and the current deterioration of the economy and culture of the United States. We now live with an unfettered acquisitional philosophy that is coupled with the advent of the technological means, via the media, to control our public assessment of its morality . . . or, in this case, the lack thereof. Public shame would once tend to control greed, but now greed has become something that is publicly acceptable or even praised.

THE TIME HAS come to refine our original revolution and break the nefarious link between our wealthy and our politicians. Not only does reversing our current devolvement into serfdom require this correction, but our very future as a species requires it. The unfettered and uncoordinated greed of the wealthy is quickly rendering our planet unfit for human habitation as they "externalize" their toxic "expenses" into our common environment.

You may think that it is in the self-interest of our wealthy overlords to govern in a way that promotes the well being of the nation as a whole; and you would be correct, that would be the sensible path to pursue. Experience has shown, however, that in the real world such enlightened self interest is rare. Our overlords are short sighted. The greed factor expressed individually invariably overrides any hope of this avaricious group working together toward common goals. The practitioners of this greed have been selected by Darwinian processes for their extreme avariciousness, not their intellect. They *cannot* work together without giving up their personal greed, at least to some extent, so they don't. The result is to render the overall management of the country impossible to accomplish in a rational fashion.

The ancient fable about the frog and the scorpion comes to mind in this context: the scorpion kills the frog who is kindly giving him a ride across a river, and thus drowns when the frog dies, simply because "it's his nature."[9] As a class, our wealthy elites have proved themselves no different from the fabled scorpion. They will kill us all, and the entire planet with us, in pursuit of their unfettered greed. In addition to this problem, there is no chance at all that any meaningful change in the current system will take place if we wait for our "representatives" to take the initiative. They are carefully selected and controlled to

---

[9]http://en.wikipedia.org/wiki/The_Scorpion_and_the_Frog

prevent exactly that. We must *force* these traitors out, and replace them with individuals who will actually represent We, the People.

THIS HANDBOOK PROPOSES a plan that is specifically targeted at the underlying root of our national problems: breaking the link between wealthy special interests and our politicians. That link is clearly money. The plan proposed is not an easy plan by any means, but it is a potentially workable plan . . . if it is actually worked by enough citizens. We, the People retain one clear advantage in this latest in a sordid and long history of class wars: despite our current fall from our former strength and honor, our country retains a heritage that was and remains a firm foundation: our Constitution. Just a few simple "tweaks" to our existing system can thwart the control our greedy masters now exercise. Just a few simple "tweaks" to refine our great original revolution and its greatest document, our Constitution, can make our nation great once again. A few simple "tweaks" to make the United States a place of true justice and equality for all. A place where the wonders of technology are harnessed for the good of all, and the profit of all . . . instead of the place our country has sadly become: a place of constant surveillance and constant control of all the "little people" to keep them orderly, and working at maximum effort for minimum pay, so the wealthy can get ever more obscenely fat at the expense of all others.

In this handbook I first propose a means of returning our electoral process to transparency and fairness in spite of all government efforts to prevent these goals, a necessary first step. I then propose three essential Constitutional amendments that are designed to solidify and enhance our emancipation from the wealthy: First, an amendment to codify and make permanent the return of our elections to fairness and transparency. Second, an amendment to eliminate political bribery by any means, especially "campaign contributions." And third, an amendment to break up obscene levels of wealth and manufacturing capital concentration that give monopoly economic power to a few, plus too much power to meddle in our yet to be realized democracy. No sane country can afford to allow "Too Big To Fail" businesses to exist. They are way too dangerous!

Chapters three and four address how to reclaim our electoral apparatus, but first it is very important that the reader clearly understand the extremely formidable obstacles to this task so they may be worked around, which is the subject of Chapter two.

Chapter 2 — A Daunting Task

A man must be far gone in Utopian speculations who can seriously doubt that, if these States should either be wholly disunited, or only united in partial confederacies, the subdivisions into which they might be thrown would have frequent and violent contests with each other. To presume a want of motives for such contests as an argument against their existence, would be to forget that men are ambitious, vindictive, and rapacious. To look for a continuation of harmony between a number of independent, unconnected sovereignties in the same neighborhood, would be to disregard the uniform course of human events, and to set at defiance the accumulated experience of ages.

Alexander Hamilton, Federalist No. 6

HAMILTON'S WORDS ABOUT frequent and violent

contests were in reference to the individual States, but apply equally to all groups of humans whatever the real or imagined grouping. We are in such a contest now: a contest between our corporations and the wealthy elite who own them, and the rest of us. This contest is without question a class war, with the wealthy attacking the middle class and the poor.

The reasons for this contest would be easily recognized by Hamilton. Our wealthy elite have come to think of themselves as distinct and separate from the "little people" at their economic feet. The wealthy feel that they are entitled by their wealth to inherent privileges conveyed by their class. They feel themselves to be aristocrats, in other words. Chief among the aristocratic privileges the wealthy feel they are entitled to is the "right" to fish in the ocean of common humanity at their economic feet in any manner they see fit; unfettered by any laws. Their point of view is not unreasonable; our wealthy elite are, in fact, above the law. They have clearly proven this fact by being allowed to nearly destroy the United States economy while extracting rapacious profits — without any legal consequence whatsoever. Moreover, our last two Presidents have demonstrated that the law does not apply to them with their illegal wars; wars pursued on behalf of their wealthy masters. Nixon claimed that: *"When the President does it, that means that it's not illegal."* The corollary to this principle is that the President, being the servant of the wealthy who enable him and also above the law, thus places the wealthy even further above the law.

Our wealthy elite have deluded themselves with the self-serving psychological trick of placing those whom they wish to live parasitically upon in a separate group: the "little people" group. This "in group, out group" mentality is used to justify the exploitation of the "out" group and to avoid any feelings of guilt. The wealthy have their own "in group," of course, to which they relate; but the vast majority of "others" are just that: others. These *others* are the fish that the wealthy happily trick and exploit with bright, shiny, lures . . . eventually feeding on their substance in a modern form of social cannibalism. Theirs is a Darwinian view featuring themselves as the "fittest," and thus justified by nature to take anything they want from the "weaker" others. Never mind the fact that the great mass of society has been systematically forced into a weak position through no fault of their own.

In our society the wealthy actually produce little or nothing, and live in a parasitic relationship on the backs of those who do. It is the "little people" who both produce the products of society, and if that society is relatively healthy, consume the far greater portion of these products. When, however, the greed and rapacious avarice of the obscenely wealthy breaks the circular nature of this process by redirecting too great a portion of a society's wealth into their own coffers, their unrestrained parasitism breaks the *entire* system. With the means of consumption subverted into hands that *cannot* consume in the quantities required to maintain the system, the system must collapse. That is the practical economic reality we currently face, but the moral implication demands equal attention.

During a time when American families have devoted an ever greater percentage of their members to the work force, often leaving their children in a stranger's care, or with no care at all; and their individual productivity has more than doubled, real family wages have remained the same or declined. That is, in the same period that the American work force doubled production per worker or more . . . their share of the *profits* from that increased production was cut in half. If each worker's share of increased production had tracked that production the mean wage of American workers would now be roughly $90,000 per year. Instead, it is roughly $52,000 per year. This while American workers put in an average of 122 more hours per year than English workers, and an average of 378 more hours per year than German workers.[10]

The share of the profits that American workers produced but did not receive was *taken* by our wealthy elites via various manipulations of the legal structure that were enacted by their political lackeys. Legal constraints on unions were extremely effective in keeping wages low. Preventing or eliminating trade controls was another, because they meant as a practical reality that a worker in the United States with high maintenance expenses (food and shelter) had to compete directly with a worker overseas that had very low maintenance expenses. Reduced taxes for themselves was another direct theft from the public treasury. *The main method our obscenely wealthy individuals used to redirect profits from the increased productivity of We, the People to themselves was to subvert the government of We, the People.*

ACCORDING TO ECONOMIST Mark J. Perry: "Between 1947 and 1980, real manufacturing output per worker doubled from $35,000 to $70,000, and since 1980 output per worker has more than doubled again to almost $150,000 per year in 2010, a new record high.[11]" While productivity per worker was doubling twice, real wages rose modestly from 1947 to 1971, but since 1971 have either stagnated or declined. In other words, at least some of the rewards for increased worker productivity were shared with the

---

[10]http://stats.oecd.org/Index.aspx?DataSetCode=ANHRS

[11]http://blog.american.com/2011/05/chart-of-the-day-manufacturing-output-per-worker-reaches-new-high-in-2010/

workers that produced that increase up until the early seventies, then the means was found to keep the rewards from further increases in productivity firmly in the hands of the obscenely wealthy. This redirection of wealth did more than rob those who actually produced it, it also took a huge portion of the money needed for the consumption side of the economic balance between manufacturing and consumption out of the economy. The United States economy is currently staggering near collapse from this problem.

If the wealthy were truly intelligent parasites they would realize that the extreme income inequality they have imposed on the United States economy is the equivalent of a farmer eating his seed corn. They are, in other words, destroying the source of their own wealth. But do not make the mistake of thinking that merely realizing that this is happening would change the outcome. The extreme greed set will always wait for "the other players" to make the necessary sacrifices. Naturally, "the other players" feel the same way.

So, where are we relative to the rest of the world in terms of income inequality? According to the CIA, with data from 136 nations available as of this writing, the result of the various manipulations our wealthy elite have made over the last several decades has been to place the United States at 97th in the world in terms of income equality. The United States is worse than Egypt. The United States is worse than Kenya. The United States is worse than Russia, China, Guyana, Nigeria, Iran — the list goes on and on.[12] But do not be concerned about our poor ranking relative to the rest of the world. American

---

[12]https://www.cia.gov/library/publications/the-world-factbook/rankorder/2172rank.html

exceptionalism remains intact. You may rest assured we remain number one in the quality and quantity of our ***ambitious, vindictive, and rapacious*** men.

AS OUR COUNTRY has aged, the situation has worsened at an accelerated rate for We, the People as our wealthy elite find and utilize ever more sophisticated means of public control. Intense study in the field of Social Psychology has provided the scientific foundation for extremely effective product advertising, for example, and this science has been very effectively applied in the political arena as well. Hamilton's ***ambitious, vindictive, and rapacious*** men apparently cannot be satisfied with the near absolute control these tools provide, however, and have now found the means to directly manipulate our elections. Computers are amazing tools that work equally well in the hands of evil people as those with benign intent. Control, and ever better control, has always been the goal of the wealthy.

Control of the *laws* of society is one of the most effective ways to maximize profits known, especially when this control is used to promote profitable wars, but control of the electoral process in a nominal democracy provides absolute control of the laws and those who make them. From the crude beginnings of a welcoming warm hearth and camaraderie as a means of controlling politicians, the wealthy have carefully developed the following formidable list of interacting social control methods:

> **Ownership of the media.** Nobody can get elected without media exposure, and anyone who "gets out of line" can be destroyed by the media. The media are controlled by the wealthy.

Candidate selection. The media and other methods of direct control over the "major political parties" allow the wealthy to select the candidates that are made available for election, destroying all those they do not approve of with lies, or simply by preventing access to media. Naturally, the wealthy prefer easily manipulable individuals such as George Walker Bush. This is why electoral "choices" in the United States have evolved to become always between some flavor of Tweedledum and Tweedledee, and the people's choice is always to pick the lessor evil between them.

A single-party system. Our so-called two-party system is a sham that has proved itself very useful for manipulating the public. "If we could just get a .... elected next time, all will be well." Right. Change you can *believe* in. Like believing in the Tooth Fairy the myth of bipartisan rancor is just that, a myth. Bipartisanship in the United States is, in fact, nearly perfect. Our "two" parties work hand in hand to implement the goals of their wealthy masters through theater.

Direct manipulation of elections. Electronic voting is completely opaque and has clearly been manipulated. Remember when discrepancies between "exit polls" and voting results were interpreted as evidence of an invalid election? Those were the good old days. At least you knew you were being screwed.

A system of bribery. Until recently, politicians got to keep any excess in their "campaign war chest" as their personal property when they retired. They passed this "privilege" into law years ago, making the acquisition of lots of money in that account very desirable; and useful for keeping their jobs as well. Now they have to be creative to accomplish the same effect: they have to pretend that the expenditures they make from their "campaign war chest" are "not for personal use."

THESE TOOLS PROVIDE the means with which our wealthy elite have stolen the wealth of We, the People. They have used them to provide favorable laws when they were needed; immunity from prosecution when immunity was required; and to promote wars by the dozens to keep the domestic fear factor nearly as high as the extreme profits made from all those expensive and non-reusable bombs. The economic results have been astounding from the perspective of everyone affected . . . just for different reasons. It is clearly time for the people of the United States to do something about our extreme embarrassment of a government, this criminal conspiracy, and live again as honorable and moral men and women. The added income a more equitable distribution of wealth will provide will also be most welcome.

UNFORTUNATELY, IN ADDITION to the various ways the wealthy steal from us, we face a much more daunting problem that originates from within. We must overcome an amazingly consistent tendency in humans to generally always obey *authority*. This tendency is exacerbated in the United States by the fact that we are a Christian nation, trusting in God and taught from childhood to be subservient to Christian Authority. Reason be damned, we have *faith*.

Edward Gibbon, in his famous *The History of the Decline and Fall of the Roman Empire*,[13] was of the opinion that a primary reason for the decline of the Roman empire was a general loss of *civic virtue* that he directly attributed to the spread of Christianity. Specifically, the belief that Christians would be virtuous and thus earn a place in heaven if they ignore the pains of the here and now and wait with piety and patience for their reward after death.[14] The practical effect of this point of view has been concisely elucidated by Napoleon[15] when he quipped that *"Religion is what keeps the poor from murdering the rich."*

Religion is always strongly promoted by our wealthy elites for obvious reasons: both to defend themselves, as Napoleon points out, and because workers who are willing to defer their pay until their check is placed in their coffin with them are cheap workers never paid who rarely complain about the swindle. The relevant point here is that religious Christians will not bestir themselves for civic virtue in the United States any more than they did in Roman lands. Thomas Jefferson explained the root of the problem this way:

> *[M]an, once surrendering his reason, has no remaining guard against absurdities the most monstrous, and like a ship without a rudder, is the sport of every wind. With such persons, gullibility which they call faith,*

---

[13]1776–88

[14]http://en.wikipedia.org/wiki/Decline_of_the_Roman_Empire#Edward_Gibbon

[15]Napoleon Bonaparte, French general & politician (1769 - 1821)

*takes the helm from the hand of reason,
and the mind becomes a wreck.*

Thomas Jefferson's letter to Rev. James Smith,
December 8, 1822

Jefferson also explains the inevitable result of such gullibility.

*But a short time elapsed after the
death of the great reformer of the
Jewish religion, before his principles
were departed from by those who
professed to be his special servants, and
perverted into an engine for enslaving
mankind, and aggrandizing their
oppressors in Church and State: that
the purest system of morals ever before
preached to man has been adulterated
and sophisticated by artificial
constructions, into a mere contrivance
to filch wealth and power to themselves:
that rational men, not being able to
swallow their impious heresies, in order
to force them down their throats, they
raise the hue and cry of infidelity,
while themselves are the greatest
obstacles to the advancement of the real
doctrines of Jesus, and do, in fact,
constitute the real Anti-Christ.*

Thomas Jefferson's letter to S. Kercheval, 1810

In 1961 the Social Psychologist Stanley Milgram performed a seminal experiment in an attempt to understand how badly people were willing to behave, just because some *authority* told them to perform a particular heinous act.[16] The results were astounding, have been repeated many times, and later confirmed by meta-analysis to apply across nearly all cultures. Dr. Milgram's results boil down to this: consistently, 61 - 66% of subjects tested will administer what they think could be a lethal electrical shock to a fellow human being, just because a man they do not know, but who is wearing a white lab coat as a badge of authority, tells them that "The experiment must go on" or something similar. Dr. Milgram explained his experimental results thusly:

> *The legal and philosophic aspects of obedience are of enormous importance, but they say very little about how most people behave in concrete situations. I set up a simple experiment at Yale University to test how much pain an ordinary citizen would inflict on another person simply because he was ordered to by an experimental scientist. Stark authority was pitted against the subjects' [participants'] strongest moral imperatives against hurting others, and, with the subjects' [participants'] ears ringing with the screams of the victims, authority won more often than not. The extreme willingness of adults to go to almost any lengths on the command of an authority constitutes the chief finding of the study and the fact most urgently demanding explanation.*

---

[16]http://en.wikipedia.org/wiki/Milgram_experiment

> *Ordinary people, simply doing their*
> *jobs, and without any particular*
> *hostility on their part, can become*
> *agents in a terrible destructive process.*
> *Moreover, even when the destructive*
> *effects of their work become patently*
> *clear, and they are asked to carry out*
> *actions incompatible with fundamental*
> *standards of morality, relatively few*
> *people have the resources needed to*
> *resist authority.*[17]

Imagine the intestinal fortitude required to defy a jack-booted authority who may also be threatening to arrest you, or gas you, or break your skull with a heavy wooden stick, or beat you silly against the hard concrete street, or even shoot you. Social control via terrorism of this sort is the stock and trade of the United States government, and many others. In Egypt roughly eight hundred fifty people were murdered by Hosni Mubarak's goons before this tyrant was overthrown, and throughout this terror the incredibly brave people of Egypt stood firm. The good news is that the people of Egypt have won their battle, and have now demanded that Mr. Mubarak be put on trial for his murders. Our friends in Egypt have proven beyond question that revolutions are *not* easy! But they have also proven that they *can* be accomplished — you just have to be smart about it — and have a lot of help. Help that comes from *organizing*, and building a core group of patriots willing to fight. Fortunately, not *all* Americans have been emasculated, just most of them.

The single most important thing that we who contemplate a few simple refinements to our original revolution

---

[17] *ibid.*

must develop in the population as a whole, is a sense of confidence. We must remind We, the People that our politicians have sworn to work for us, not the other way around. We are, however, a beaten and terrorized people here in the self-proclaimed "Land of the Brave and Home of the Free." We have also been systematically conditioned to think of ourselves as helpless. Our government spies on us constantly, and intimidates us with laws giving them the "right" to throw any one of us in jail indefinitely for no reason, or torture us, or execute us. All this without any judicial review whatsoever, or legal consequence for the guilty.

We have sunk that low! If you think I'm engaged in hyperbole, just remember that Osama bin Laden was executed without trial or charge. I say "executed" because I simply don't believe that three Navy Seals could not subdue him when they found him unarmed, as he apparently was. In contrast, shortly after bin Laden was murdered the Serbian government sent the *police* to capture Ratko Mladic, who was reported to have two pistols in his possession when he was accosted. Are we to believe that the Serbian police are more skilled than the members of Seal Team Six? Mladic was captured, essentially without incident, and the Serbian government now plans to send him to The Hague to be tried for war crimes. This is what *should* have happened to Osama bin Laden, but *perhaps his testimony would have proved too embarrassing for some high ranking Americans.*

In addition to bin Laden, President Obama has also issued an execution order on an American citizen living in Yemen, Anwar al-Awlaki, and has already made one attempt to kill him,[18] also without trial or any judicial

---

[18]http://www.salon.com/news/opinion/glenn_greenwald/

review. Meanwhile, confessed war criminals, George W. Bush and Dick Cheney, remain free, as do the perpetrators of our current economic meltdown. Not only are we being robbed and subjected to a class war, our entire upper class of society has elevated themselves above the law. They are lawless, and they don't care if we know it. In fact, they want us to know it for the intimidation that knowledge provides.

Chapter 3 —
Transparent Elections

Everyone is entitled to their own opinion, but not their own facts.

Daniel Patrick Moynihan

FOR THE REASONS given above and more, I repeat that the single most important thing that we must do to save our country is to build the confidence in We, the People that enables them to stand up and resist the criminal conspiracy we sadly refer to as the United States Government. To build this confidence we need to identify and focus upon an issue that a very high percentage of our fellow Americans will currently recognize as their unequivocal right, but which they are in fact currently being deprived of. Fortunately, the ideal issue has been provided to us by our government, gift wrapped with a fancy bow. That issue is voter fraud. Not the imaginary voter fraud the Republicans scream about and use to suppress voter registration wherever they can, but *government* voter fraud.

There is no right to vote in the Constitution. Our almost universally presumed right to vote has been obtained through suffrage battles and amendments to the Constitution. Most importantly, however, and the issue here, is the overlooked fact that the right to vote implies the more specific right to *have your vote counted and recognized* in a way so obviously transparent that there is no question it has been *fairly* counted. *This* right does not currently exist in the United States except in isolated pockets. *This* issue will resonate widely with We, the People, and will be very difficult for our government to argue against without revealing that their real intent is to *prevent* fair elections and transparent counting.

WE GIVE PUBLIC lip service to being a democracy and supporting democratic ideals when, in fact, our government has done everything in its power to subvert any vestige of democracy around the world and at home.[19] We have never been a democracy in the United States, of course, but a republic. Still, the days when we could democratically elect our representatives have long passed. The advent of widespread electronic voting has removed any residual vestige of transparency from our elections, and we now have no way at all to know what happens to our votes once cast. This fact has been well elaborated and documented elsewhere[20] and I will not spend more time upon this issue here.

THE ONLY REASON we do not have transparent and fair elections in the United States is because *our politicians do not want transparent and fair elections and have made every effort to prevent them.* Almost every country in the world refuses to acquiesce to the desires of

---

[19]See, for example, Naomi Klein's *"The Shock Doctrine, the Rise of Disaster Capitalism."*

[20]See, for example, the HBO special *"Hacking Democracy"* which can be viewed here: http://video.google.com/videoplay?docid=7926958774822130737#
And also http://www.blackboxvoting.org/

such politicians, and manages to have transparent elections with paper ballots in spite of their politicians efforts to prevent them. These countries wisely refuse to acquiesce because their own hard experience has shown that the United States has no monopoly on the **ambitious, vindictive, and rapacious** men Hamilton describes. Experience worldwide thus suggests the following maxim: *If the means to cheat with an election are available, cheating will be done.* Paper ballots are the obvious answer to this problem. Properly done, an election performed with paper ballots is completely transparent because almost anyone can understand paper, pens, and the meaning of marks on a ballot. The real issue is "transparency." Very few people understand computers,[21] or electronic voting machines, thus leaving us all in the position of *trusting* them when they are used for elections. Experience worldwide has shown very clearly, however, that trust is not a good idea when politicians are involved.

In fact, the way we do elections in the United States, with electronic voting, is worse than trusting politicians. We have been forced, by our government, to trust computers running proprietary, secret software that is owned, provided, and controlled by people with a strong interest in the outcome of our elections. Call me cynical, but in my view this practice is not a good idea. I don't believe that I'm alone in that view, and this fact can be used to double advantage. First, as mentioned above, it is very difficult for anyone to openly oppose honest elections; and second, should honest elections actually become common in the United States they would make it possible to throw the despicable scum we now have holding political offices

---

[21]And those who *do* understand them *do not* trust them for electoral purposes.

out of those offices.

Imagine the following situation: There is an election, and at almost every precinct the usual electronic systems are used in the "official" voting places. The electoral business as usual, in other words. This election will be different, however. In the parking lots just outside of these "official" voting establishments, or in nearby buildings, groups of citizens will set up their own facilities to mirror the official election in as many precincts as possible, but with this critical difference: *every effort will be made to make the "mirror" election completely and obviously transparent, fair, and capable of being documented as such for all concerned.* This mirror election will be performed without asking for official permission. Why should we citizens need to ask for permission to audit our politicians? All the voters who vote at the "official" sites will be politely asked to repeat their vote at the "mirror" sites, and also to sign affidavits to the effect that they are legally registered voters and have cast the exact same vote in both instances. Paper ballots will be used in the unofficial sites, and will be marked with permanent ink pens. If possible, voter registrations will be meticulously checked in all cases.

Multiple witnesses will watch everything. The entire proceeding will be videotaped and streamed live on the Internet for others to watch and record, and the ballot box into which voters drop their ballot will be a large, heavy, transparent plastic box in the middle of the room where everyone and the cameras can continually watch it. At the close of voting all ballots will be immediately counted publicly, at least three times by a minimum of three separate human counters for each issue, with witnesses and cameras observing. When the counts are completed, all witnesses will sign an affidavit attesting to the honesty of the election. The results and the witness affidavit will be copied and handed out to any interested parties present, as well as posted on the Internet *before* the witnesses leave and the "mirror" site closes shop for the night. This is just a brief description[22], but I think you must agree that done properly, the results from this "mirror" site would represent voter intent unambiguously and transparently, and *the voters themselves will recognize this fact simply from experiencing the process.* This exercise is both a means to a specific end: transparent and fair elections; and it is a teaching method that demonstrates to the public what can and should be done.

Now one of two things will result, either of which will be in favor of We, the People. Either the results from the "official" voting and the "mirror" voting will match, thus providing verification that the election was accurate in the particular precincts mirrored, or the results will prove discrepant. If the results are discrepant, the same good citizens who set up and ran the mirror site can attempt to go to court and make the case that the official results do not reflect the voter's will. They will have an extremely sound case that will be viewed by officialdom as a serious threat. But I say attempt, because it is likely that the courts will find some reason to deny "standing" or find some other excuse to deny such a hearing. The election officials will certainly not want to have their election effort challenged, because they have *no* way to prove that their electronic vote tallies reflect voter intent, and will almost certainly fight any effort to test this issue.

Do not think for a minute that such a rejection by the courts is a loss, because it is in fact a win! Now you have a clear issue before the people who voted, people in large numbers who will clearly know that the "mirror"

---

[22]Details may be found in Chapter 7

results are far more transparent, and thus far more likely to be honest, than the "official" results. And yet, they will be told by their "officials" that the obviously incorrect tally that they obtained is "really" the "correct" one! "*You must trust us! We are OFFICIALS!*" they will loudly claim. The election officials will thus be forced into the same unenviable situation Groucho Marx occupied when he proclaimed: "*Who are you going to believe, me or your lying eyes?*"

There is only one way that the people who voted in both elections can reasonably view such a result from the courts: as being "officially" denied their democracy, which will in fact be the exact case. The difference will be that all the excuses given about various "problems" with the electronic voting machines, while insisting on continuing to use their results, will very obviously boil down to this unequivocal message from our officials: "*We don't mind you voting, we just don't want you to be able to have your vote counted or recognized. So just settle down like good docile citizen-cattle and go home to your TV for a quick brain wash. You'll feel better after another dose of intellectual pabulum.*"

This implied response serves our purpose well, because it will raise citizen awareness, and it will raise a strong righteous anger. Both reactions are more than merely useful in the present context, they are required and can be exploited to correct the basic problem of rigged elections that are rigged by our government. Even if the results from the two voting sites exactly match each other, the obvious transparency of the "mirror" site will psychologically prevail as the "real" election against which the "official" election is compared in almost everyone's mind, despite the protests of officialdom that theirs is "perfectly all right."

Currently, most citizens do not believe that "their" government is manipulating elections. Some may dismiss all efforts to teach them what a transparent election can be, despite your every effort. Invincible ignorance is far from uncommon. But I cannot believe that those who do make a habit of slavishly bowing down to "authority" will amount to a high percentage in *this* case. How could such individuals justify opposing an effort to have a *demonstrably* honest election as opposed to one based purely upon trust? Should you run into one of these people nonetheless, just point out that the electronic machines cost them thousands of dollars apiece, but the printed ballots are far cheaper. Ask them to be fiscally responsible if they can't be patriotic and virtuous citizens.

As an issue to kick off a revolution electronic voting machines could not be more perfect. At every branch in this effort, the resulting path can be turned to the advantage of We, the People over the "official" blockade. Our officials might claim it's illegal to have a mirror election, or even send the police to rough you up and throw you in jail to prevent such a thing. Get video of it all, and stream it to the public on the Internet! The more the government fights this effort, the more they will lose status in the public eye and reveal themselves openly as *Gestapo* type thugs who do not work for We, the People. This perception is very dangerous for any government, and they know it. No government, no matter how vicious and how entrenched can survive without a minimum of public cooperation. If the government recognizes this peril and doesn't fight, then you will succeed in providing transparent elections. If they fight you on this issue they prove themselves the lackeys of those who don't want fair elections. Either way the People win, because in the latter instance our hidden enemy is revealed; and this enemy is inherently weak. It is a parasitic enemy that gets its strength from We, the People exclusively, and We, the People can refuse to provide that strength.

In point of fact, the only way to lose this initial battle is by refusing to engage in it and carry it through. Americans have been taught since they were infants that the United States is a democracy. They will not take kindly to finding out that it isn't, and that gets them on your side. If you demonstrate actual transparent and honest elections to them, then you have effectively won that particular battle, because *even without official cooperation, if your transparent elections are massive enough the results from them can be crammed down the official throats of our politicians simply by refusing to cooperate with the "official" results. In this way the public can "throw the bastards out" who have been destroying this country in service to their wealthy masters.* This latter effort will, of course, require some street work, but the issue is so clear I repeat: the only way to fail is to not engage the fight. Many Americans are craven, to be sure, but many more are not and will fight if clearly called upon. When you do prevail, you will demonstrate without equivocation that *We, the People, can* **force** *our will upon our government.* And not only force our will upon them, but do so in a manner that they will clearly recognize as potentially an extreme personal danger. Our politicians could certainly use a good dose of fear to get them working for We, the People instead of their far weaker wealthy masters.

ONCE CONFIDENCE IS established by We, the People, the rest becomes relatively easy. *I repeat redundantly: our government could not have provided a better issue than their damnable electronic voting machines with which to hoist them on their own proverbial petards.*

Ah, but there is that Tweedledum and Tweedledee issue which we need to address next.

Chapter 4 — Actual Debates!

Political language — and with variations this is true of all political parties, from Conservatives to Anarchists — is designed to make lies sound truthful and murder respectable, and to give an appearance of solidity to pure wind.

George Orwell, 1946

THERE WAS A time when political oratory actually dealt with substance — at least occasionally. Empty slogans like "*Change you can believe in*" were more honestly presented as actual promises, rarely kept: "*I will put a chicken in every pot if you elect me!*" Not that the Hopey Changey President seems to worry about *keeping* any promises he may have slipped and made. In any case, how nice it would be if we were able to watch real debates with real issues being debated for a real *change* with *hope*. A nice messy affair where real people put their actual thoughts forward, and anyone can play. This, of course, could not involve the mass media in any way, because the owners of the mass media certainly do not want

We, the People honestly addressing relevant issues. That would be against their interests.

But who needs the mass media? The mass media serves the interests of the wealthy exclusively. The *only* function of the mass media is to deliver the attention of We, the People into the hands of mass marketers and political manipulators. Once we retake our government some simple laws can be implemented to remind the owners of these media of some relevant facts. Facts like who owns the airwaves and the right-of-ways for their cables, and the responsibilities to the public this ownership implies. In the meantime, there's the wonderful Internet, full of amazing promise.

THERE ARE THREE issues that must be addressed to implement a series of public debates: who participates in these debates, how the debates are physically presented, and how the "winner" is selected by the public. The first problem has a long history of solutions from various sports that first compete locally, then perhaps regionally, then by county, by state and finally in the country as a whole. These techniques can be borrowed. The target is to develop a public system, starting, say, at the county level, whereby absolutely any qualified individual can realistically run for any public office; up to and including for President of the United States. The actual method used at the county level should be left to the residents of the particular county; with the only requirements being that the method used be inclusive, open, and fair.

At this point in our technological development, almost everyone has access to the Internet, either at home or in some public institution such as a library. The technologies for streaming images and audio in real time over the Internet have become very mature, and are readily available.

On the Internet here are no bottlenecks such as CBS, or FOX, or NBC, etc. from whom permission to use facilities must be obtained or to whom money must be provided. There are also an effectively unlimited number of "channels" on the Internet. As I asked above, *Who needs the mass media?* We can do things on the Internet that the mass media can only dream of, and **we can do them at little or no cost**. Besides, it will be such a pleasure to just bypass the mass media and render them irrelevant instead of the dangerous and stupefying influence they are now. They certainly deserve our disdain; for their role in promoting illegal wars for resource theft if nothing else.

ASSUME, AS AN example, that the election is for the office of President of the United States, and assume further that it is desirable to select from the widest possible set of candidates, which would be the set of potential candidates specified in Article II, Section 1 of the United States Constitution:

> *No person except a natural born Citizen, or a Citizen of the United States, at the time of the Adoption of this Constitution, shall be eligible to the Office of President; neither shall any Person be eligible to that Office who shall not have attained to the Age of thirty-five Years, and been fourteen Years a Resident within the United States.*

This particular subset of the population can be presumed to be distributed more or less equally across the country, so we need to make the entire country accessible to the process that follows. We, the People want the best possible person running the ship of state; *not* the person most willing to sell our assets to special interests cheaply, which is *always* the person supported by those special interests. We particularly do *not* want those same special interests to be able to influence candidate selection, for example via their mass media. The mass media will, of course, do what they can to promote their own interests with the usual lies. Anticipating this effort, it would be wise to set up a "fact check" site to counter both the lies of candidates and the mass media.

There are 3,143 counties, or county equivalents, in the United States. Starting at the county level we may proceed as follows: citizens living in each of these counties that meet the qualifications cited above, and want to take on the job of President, could in every instance make their case to their fellow county citizens via the Internet. Citizens could then vote for the person they prefer via the method described above and in Chapter seven. To put the problem simply; if a county can organize a series of basketball games to select the best team in the county, it ought to be able to select the best candidate for President from among its citizens. The act of doing so is itself an important step in building confidence, and will act to sort those who "can do" from those who always wait for Mr. Somebody Else to step forward. Mr. Else is a true citizen exactly because he *is* willing to step up and work the problem. Those who wait passively fail the citizenship test — and in most cases are the problem.

At each step of a series of debates the best candidate needs to be selected. This requirement defines a good place to start the process of educating the general population about how to have transparent elections; by having them to select the debate winners! For the educational value alone it is extremely valuable to have all voting at each stage of debate done as described in Chapters three and seven. As we shall see below, this would only involve six separate elections from county level to President. This is not too difficult a task, given the rewards; and keep in mind the fact that we strive toward multiple goals: to have real debates, to select candidates, to demonstrate transparent and fair elections, and most importantly, *to build confidence and civic virtue.* These are the keys to a revolutionary reformation of our country.

ONCE EACH COUNTY has selected its best candidate, preferably via Internet debates and transparent voting, then the winning county level candidates from seven adjacent counties can have the next public debates over the Internet, and the process can be repeated. Each candidate can participate in the debates from wherever he can get access to the Internet, so no real expenses are involved; and even though there will be 449 of these debates going on at roughly the same time nationally, our wonderful Internet can easily stream them all on 449 individual "channels." That way, the citizens of each group of seven counties can watch their own debates. At the end of these debates (and there is no reason debates for multiple offices can't be held), the public from the seven counties involved in each case can vote for their favorite candidate. At the end of these elections there will be 449 candidates nationwide (3143/7=449) still running for President, with each candidate representing a particular group of seven adjacent counties.

Four hundred forty nine is a prime number, but four hundred fifty may be evenly divided by fifty. So, in forty nine cases groups of nine adjacent seven county groups, plus one group of eight counties, would each have their debates, and the associated elections held at the end of these debates. This stage of the process would reduce the number of possible candidates for president to fifty.

Now ten more debates of five candidates each will get us down to ten candidates, and two more debates of five candidates each will produce two possible finalists. If you look back over the above you will see that once each county level finalist has been determined, there are only four more steps to get down to two candidates.

It will be imperative to pre-assign the county groupings and meta groupings before any debates take place, with "most adjacent" being the criterion of choice. This pre-assignment of groupings serves two important purposes: 1) It allows the "winner" at each stage to remain within his original region, which simply becomes broader at each stage, and thus regional loyalties are maintained. 2) There will inevitably be varying levels of candidate "quality" in different groupings. For example the first grouping of seven counties could easily see one such group of seven with seven superb individual candidates, one of which is the winner, then competing with the adjacent group of seven county candidates with seven very poor candidates with an eventual winner. If no gerrymandering has taken place, and how could it if adjacency by county is the criterion used, then all of this washes out in the end.

Once down to two candidates, I would suggest bundling winner "A" as the presidential candidate with winner "B" as the vice-presidential candidate on one ticket; and the reverse arrangement on a second ticket for another election prior to the final Presidential election. These two finalists are bound to be excellent candidates, the only issue is which should run for President and which Vice-President. You do not want both to run independently, as this dilutes the votes, and our wealthy masters will, no doubt, have their Tweedledum and Tweedledee candidates in competition. Having come up "through the ranks," however, with a process such as described here, there will have been quite a bit of interest developed in the outcome of We, the People's efforts, and quite a bit of active participation in the process. It is hard to imagine that these candidates will not have a great advantage over the Republican and Democratic hopefuls. The public at large will have been subjected to quite an education by this process as well, and by this time should recognize the Republicans and Democrats as the Fascists they are.

The Internet makes this sort of thing possible. This whole process could be set up so that a potential candidate could go through the entire set of debates from his own computer at near zero expense, with his "campaign headquarters" in his bedroom. There are plenty of patriotic programmers who could and would set up a system such as this. Our Fascists will hate this idea bitterly because it completely bypasses their carefully set up choke points (the media and money), and therein lies the best argument of all that it is a good system.

Chapter 5 — Citizen Referenda and Initiatives

> *The ultimate measure of a man is
> not where he stands in moments of
> comfort and convenience, but where he
> stands at times of challenge and
> controversy.*

Dr. Martin Luther King Jr.

ONCE TRANSPARENT AND fair elections have been secured it will be time to solidify them in law and to address the primary factors that brought our country to its current sorry state in the first place. Those factors boil down to two interrelated phenomena directly related to government election fraud: political bribery and the runaway capitalism that supports this bribery. The suggested amendments to the United States Constitution in Chapters seven, eight, and nine are specifically designed to address these problems.

Many states have provisions for citizen referenda or initiatives built into their constitutions. Referenda and initiatives are mechanisms by which citizens can place issues such as constitutional amendments directly onto the ballot, often in spite of government wishes. So, for example, any of the proposed amendments to the United States Constitution contained in this handbook could also be put on the ballot in many states. Doing so is without question valuable. A federal congress with nearly half of its members restricted to honest behavior by state laws — would be a significant improvement! Referenda and initiative details for individual states may be found at http://www.iandrinstitute.org/statewide_i%26r.htm.

TYPICALLY, ALL THAT is required to put an issue or amendment on a state ballot is the initial registration of the effort with the state government, and then the collection of some specific number of signatures in support of that effort. Usually a *lot* of signatures, as politicians generally don't like it when the citizens they pretend to represent tell them what to do.

All of the strategies in this Handbook require massive organization. In fact, I am writing this Handbook precisely in the hope that it will inspire exactly that kind of organizing. Fortunately, an organization initially directed at cleaning up our voting procedures will necessarily be large enough to easily accomplish the footwork necessary to get the three amendments this Handbook is promoting on state ballots where provision is in place for doing so. Moreover, given enough people willing to apply pressure to their state legislature with demonstrations, etc., *all* states are vulnerable to this approach. All states have the means via their legislative bodies to sponsor amendments to their constitution, however most politicians will probably require a strong "incentive" to actually do it.

The amendments in question: in support of transparent elections, against bribery, and to break up "too big to fail" businesses, all have inherent "curb appeal." A high percentage of our citizens will support these efforts, if they are explained to them. Publicly providing those explanations can also provide an opportunity for some fun. For example, forcing your state representative or senator to explain why he's *against* an amendment that targets political bribery could be great fun at a local "town hall" meeting.

Chapter 6 — "Don't waste any time in mourning. Organize!"

Joe Hill, November 19, 1915, just prior to his execution by firing squad. Joe Hill's last word was *"FIRE!"*[23]

ORGANIZING WE, THE People is an essential task that will determine our success, or failure. Organizing within the current political milieu is, however, on one hand, not an easy task. Americans are a people who have seen their incomes diminish and their freedoms perish. Typically, every member of a family who can must work outside the home; and way too often must work killing hours. The science of public manipulation known as "marketing" has convinced too many people to buy and consume a plethora of useless products. The same science is used for political manipulations, and in that area the "products" are worse than useless. We, the People have exchanged a firm foundation upon which to base our existence for pretty beads and gewgaws.

First the family caretakers were taken off that important job and put into the work force, just to keep up with

[23]http://en.wikipedia.org/wiki/Joe_Hill

an unrealistic perception pushed by the marketers of "how things should be." Then, as the economic squeeze tightened around We, the People, second mortgages were taken out to finance an ever more enslaving level of consumption. This increased consumption was facilitated by a "housing bubble" manipulated into existence by our Banksters. Now that tactic has collapsed, and our supposed representatives in government have effectively borrowed money from the wealthy, by selling them bonds, in order to give this borrowed money back to those very same wealthy to "bail them out" of the problems they created — because they are "*Too Big to Fail.*" Thus our "representatives" in government have put us all, plus our future generations, under crushing debt rather than punish their supporters for their crimes. Or tax them in order to fix the problems they created. In the meantime, the credit cards of We, the People, have been maxed out almost universally. Through all this, our Banksters have used trickery and fraud to gain control of the financial assets of the country until now over 40% of our national wealth is in the form of "financial instruments" which amount to liens on our collective lives; but are, in fact, nothing but words on paper. Imagine how different our economy would be if the value represented by that intrinsically useless paper was in the form of manufacturing tools that We, the People could use to create *real* wealth that was intrinsically nourishing or useful!

As a people, we are worn out. Too many people have given up all hope to want to participate in any new "organization." They simply don't have the time or the energy, and in their weakened condition they have become addicted to the soporific of mass media "entertainment" so they won't have to consider any such idea. We collectively watch "reality" shows in order to avoid reality.

On the other hand, desperate times are an organizer's best friend. Hunger and homelessness tend to wake the mentally lethargic from their natural complacency. In this regard, the Republican party has been doing a great job in Wisconsin and other states to demonstrate their plan to subject us all to abject serfdom without collective bargaining, Medicare, or Social Security. Their clear message to "throw Grandma under the bus" in the name of "fiscal responsibility" has been correctly perceived by many, and that perception has served the useful function of awakening them.

The people who run our government do not want you to organize. They hate collective bargaining about anything because it interferes with their influx of bribes. Collective bargaining also demonstrates a phenomenon they don't want demonstrated: that We, the People have power. Our politician's masters become grumpy and stingy if such things are allowed to happen. Masses of people demonstrating against the lucrative methods the wealthy dream up to screw us all will not be welcomed with open arms. So, be assured that your efforts to organize, *especially* for transparent elections, will meet legal barriers first, and the use of violence second.

Laws come in two basic forms: laws that increase the well being and freedom of almost everyone in some way, and laws that reduce the well being and freedom of most people for some minority's benefit. As long as laws increase the well being and freedom of the greater part of society, they are good laws. An example of this is the traffic law that says: "*Thou shalt drive upon the right side of the road.*" This law, which at first analysis appears to restrict the freedom of the individuals it is applied to, actually increases the freedom of all. Imagine the chaos that would result if it did not exist!

Laws that do not increase the freedom or well being of the greater part of society are clearly bad laws and should be removed. For example, laws that provide the mechanisms that allow large corporations to avoid almost all taxes are clearly bad laws for a society to have. These are the laws that some sleazy politician sold in the process of whoring for his or her wealthy masters. Washington's infamous 14th street whores are more honorable. They, at least, sell a service they own. Our politicians sell *our* property. The point I am trying to make here is that when laws are used to impede your organizing you may rest assured that they are there for the benefit of those who don't want you organizing, not the benefit of We, the People. In my view, that fact gives you the moral right to circumvent these laws in any way you can.

The traditional government (corporate) answer to union organizing or the union strikes that may result has been to use terror tactics. The owners of the corporations being struck pay their government thugs to break up the strikers; usually with payments direct to political "campaign funds." The government then supplies the muscle and the terror. Machine guns have been used against women and children in union camps. The man quoted in the chapter heading, Joe Hill, was a union organizer likely framed for murder by our government and executed.[24] Overall, the level of government violence used against union organizations has been sordid and constant. (For a particularly chilling description of one instance of this violence read the account of "The Ludlow Massacre" pointed to in this footnote.[25]) Your efforts to organize honest elections will be viewed much more severely than mere union organiz-

---

[24]http://en.wikipedia.org/wiki/Joe_Hill
[25]http://libcom.org/history/1914-the-ludlow-massacre

ing, because yours has the potential to completely pull the props out from under a very profitable criminal enterprise: our government!

Assuming you still have a burning urge to actually do something effective like organizing to *force* honest elections, here are a few steps to take. First, and most importantly, you must educate yourself about how our current system works and how it evolved. I strongly recommend the following books:

1. Zinn, Howard, *et al.*; '*Voices of a People's History of the United States*'

2. Zinn, Howard; '*A People's History of the United States*'

3. Klein, Naomi; '*The Shock Doctrine: The Rise of Disaster Capitalism*'

Next, find your local union halls and go to some meetings. See if they will let you make a presentation to explain what you are trying to do, and why. The unions are your natural ally, and should be willing to help. Most of the union members are quite cognizant of the way they have been robbed, but be aware of the fact that some union leaders may have been subverted and are actually working for company management.

It's a bit of a long shot, but you might also want to try visiting various political party meetings. Most counties have political "Executive Committees," for example the Democratic Executive Committee and the equivalent Republican Executive Committee. There may be a Green party equivalent as well. Ask if you may address them. I was a member of my local Democratic Executive Committee before I became too disgusted with them to continue, so I know positively that quite a few genuinely concerned, and very frustrated, individuals may be found there. There might even be a few such individuals at a Republican Executive Committee meeting . . .

Use the blogs on the Internet!

If you go down this road I think I can guarantee you will soon meet like minded people. They are everywhere, and everywhere as frustrated as you. Eventually, someone with the necessary skills will put up a web site to be used as a central information clearing house. Will that be you? If not, and in the meantime, remember that "All Politics Are Local."

Chapter 7 — An Amendment Requiring Transparent Elections

JOINT RESOLUTION

Proposing an amendment to the Constitution defining the method by which the people of the United States shall conduct elections.

Resolved by the Senate and House of Representatives of the United States of America in Congress assembled (two-thirds of each House concurring therein), That the following article is proposed as an amendment to the Constitution, which shall be valid to all intents and purposes as part of the Constitution when ratified by the legislatures of three-fourths of the several States.

ARTICLE _____

"The right of citizens of the United States to transparent and fair elections shall not be denied or abridged by the United States or by any State for any reason.

"All elections conducted under the auspices of the United States shall be conducted with paper ballots, said ballots to be marked by hand with an indelible marking device, accumulated in public view, and subsequently counted in public view, without any break in public view, until such time that all tallies are completed and publicly posted from each polling place individually.

"All count tallies are to be publicly posted by all available means in such a form that they can be aggregated by any interested citizen.

"Provision shall be made to accommodate all interested electoral witnesses, up to twenty five witnesses per polling place. Witnesses must be citizens of the polling district, or members of groups overseeing election integrity, or otherwise have a direct interest in the polling, such as representing a candidate seeking election.

"Three individuals, all citizens of the polling district, shall be appointed as individuals responsible for the integrity and safety of all ballots during polling and for a minimum of one year after polling, and for jointly making available to any interested parties the ballots themselves for counting in their presence throughout the year should this counting be requested. Congress shall compensate these responsible citizens as appropriate, and provide the best technical means available to them for protecting ballot integrity. Any failure to protect the integrity of polled ballots entrusted to all three responsible citizen's joint care shall be punishable by imprisonment for a minimum of one year for each count. Such punishment to be

applied equally to all three responsible citizens.

(Signed)

Speaker of the House of Representatives.

(Signed)

*Vice President of the United States and
President of the Senate.*

Hamilton's **ambitious, vindictive, and rapacious** men are highly concentrated in the field of politics, for the obvious reason that it is much easier to legislate wealth for yourself via the paybacks provided by the wealthy than it is to work for it. Such men will view the theft of an election as encumbered by a slight risk, but completely without moral issue. So, for hundreds of years our politicians have been finding various ways to circumvent voter intent. When paper ballots were the only technology available, the ballot boxes would be stuffed, or counted in secret and the favored result subsequently published. The mechanical voting machines in use prior to the advent of electronic machines could have their mechanical counters set at any desired starting point in order to produce the desired result. Punch cards could simply be replaced with pre-punched cards that gave the desired result. In short, some means was always gamed into the system to allow for vote tally manipulation if at all possible. In each case those responsible for the fraud would intentionally "not understand" the problem with the method used, or deny it existed. The challenge for us is to design a voting system so utterly transparent that it becomes undeniable that the results of an election truly and accurately reflect voter intent.

The Greeks had a near foolproof system: all the electors would gather, each having previously obtained a few white and black rocks to be used for each election. If the issue in question required a "Yes" a white stone signified it, if a "No" a black stone was used. A pot or similar container would be displayed and upended to show it was empty. Then the electors would line up and one by one toss a single rock into the pot. This is where the term "casting a vote" originates. All others could hear the rock as it dropped and confirm that only one rock was dropped. At the end of voting, the pot was emptied, the rocks separated by color, and counted as the electors watched. This was a *transparently* fair election! If there was any question of that, the total number of stones in the pot could be compared to the number of electors to unveil any trickery.

There is more at stake here than merely assuring that elections are honest. Of course we cannot break the hold our wealthy elite have on our government without this first step of assuring honest elections, but I hope you will consider the following reasons to clean up our electoral process as well.

> **1.** We are now engaged in multiple illegal wars of aggression and plunder. In every case these wars are taking place in order to steal resources (usually oil, but also rare earths, lithium, etc. in Afghanistan), or secure trade routes (an oil pipeline through Afghanistan to Pakistan), or simply to use up munitions and increase the bottom line for the manufacturers of these materials. In other words, these wars are all about plundering in one form or another. Hun-

dreds of thousands of innocent people have been and are being killed; by us, the people of the United States, and the very land under these wars is being rendered uninhabitable forever by our heinous practice of disposing of our depleted uranium[26] on it. Uranium that has had most of the fissionable isotopes extracted for use in nuclear reactors or weapons, but is still horridly poisonous, is being used as munitions in these lands. Depleted uranium munitions vaporize and burn upon impact and thus scatter this long term death beyond any possibility of recovery. Depleted uranium munitions will remain radioactive with a half-life of over four billion years. The practice of using depleted uranium as a war material is perhaps the most heinous crime ever perpetrated by members of our species, bar none. On the "heinous" scale — we are very clearly *"number one."*

For this reason and too many others, it has been argued by many of those in the lands affected by our aggression and looting that *all* Americans are now legitimate targets for retribution. It is argued that we are all legitimate targets because we twice *elected* George W. Bush, and once elected Barack Obama, the current direct perpetrators of these crimes. Bush and Obama, who, in the eyes of the world, represented or represent the *people* of the United States exactly because *we are viewed as having actively elected* them.

---

[26]http://en.wikipedia.org/wiki/Depleted_uranium

As a people we certainly are guilty of passively allowing these crimes to proceed, but I would argue that we *did not* elect the people directly responsible for them. Our representatives were forced upon us. Our electoral system has been a complete sham since electronic voting machines have been crammed down our collective throats. Moreover, *Being forced into a position of picking the lessor of two preselected evils is not a legitimate election, even if the voting is honest.* We absolutely must demonstrate this point to the world by correcting the fundamental problems with our elections and by shipping those directly responsible for the atrocities committed in our name to The Hague for trial. If we do not do this, our guilty verdict from the perspective of the rest of the world will stand, and justly so. Our failure to act in this matter will confirm the legitimacy of our status as targets.

2. There is a near zero possibility of breaking the stranglehold our wealthy elite hold on our government without honest elections. The only practical alternative is violent open rebellion. Moreover, it will be difficult enough to break this stranglehold with honest elections. Americans are typically forthright individuals who would not lie or steal from anyone — and that makes it very difficult for them to understand sociopathic individuals who will. Sociopaths do exist, however. And when these sociopaths control the means of public communication, the mass media, they can lie with impunity and use various tricks like "special pleading" to obfuscate any issue and to generally confuse the public into accepting their point of view. For example, consider this common lie: "*We can't tax the rich. We need them to be rich so the trickle down from their activity floats us all up.*" To paraphrase a joke from the "The Daily Show" with Jon Steward: That "trickle down" is actually a massive yellow deluge from on high, pounding us all down into the dirt. A strangely hot deluge with a familiar and repugnant smell.

3. The fight for honest elections is winnable, and clearly righteous. The harder the fight is to win, the more righteous it will appear to the general public, and therefore the more support it will have. This fight is where the confidence for fighting further issues like getting the amendments listed in this Handbook passed will originate. It is a national issue that can be addressed locally, and it is the foundational organizing principle upon which to base all that follows.

As with the Greek election method described above, a transparent election boils down to the following simple principle:

Every step of the election process must be publicly viewable and verifiable, except the value of the actual vote cast (which rock is dropped), right up to and including the counting and the public posting of tallies.

What follows is one method to accomplish a transparent and fair election:

1. Upon arrival at the polling place, preferably a single large room, a potential voter must show identification to confirm he or she is a registered voter. An Internet based database can then be consulted to verify that this particular person has not already voted in some other precinct. If this hurdle is passed, the voter is given a ballot with a tear-off top that is printed with a unique human *and* computer readable "serial number." This number is assigned to the voter, and also to an Internet based database that "checks off" that particular voter as in possession of this particular ballot. The ballot itself should be printed on one side only and be made of heavy card stock. The blank ballot should be presented to the voter with a large paper clip. As will be shown below, this procedure will prevent multiple voting, and is fairly typical of existing systems.

2. The voter may then proceed to a space with a table and visual shields designed to preclude anyone from seeing his or her marks, to mark the ballot with his or her choices. Should the voter make a mistake, the ballot can be returned, it's serial number entered into the computer system as invalid, and the ballot exchanged for a new, blank ballot. The old ballot should be stamped with an "invalid" mark, in front of the person returning it and the witnesses, and both it and its attached serial number retained.

3. Once the voter is satisfied that his or her ballot is marked as intended, he or she may fold it once, use the paper clip to keep it folded, and proceed to the ballot box. The ballot box should be ruggedly constructed of clear plastic; be of large capacity, say a cube three feet on a side, with a padlocked hinged top containing a slot sufficiently large for a ballot to be easily inserted, but no more. This ballot box should be in a clear area with a minimum of ten feet of empty space on all horizontal sides; with this clear area delineated by rope barriers similar to those used in theaters to guide crowds. At the entrance to this enclosure, an election worker can ask the voter to fold back the serial number from his ballot and place it under a scanner to be scanned. This scanner should be set up to verify that this is a valid ballot via the Internet database, and to activate a large green light if it is, or a red light if it is not. If the light is green, the voter may be invited to remove his serial number from his ballot and proceed to the ballot box and drop his ballot within. If the light is red, the voter can be directed to an election official to sort out the problem *without* the ballot going into the ballot box.

All aspects of the voting should be recorded electronically with video and sound, with this record simultaneously streamed on the Internet for anyone who wishes to record and store as well as watch in real time. At least two cameras should be used to observe the ballot box throughout the proceeding. Multiple witnesses should also be present.

4. At the close of voting, tables should be arranged in a line near the ballot box, in full view of the cameras recording the election and streaming to the Internet, and with comfortable chairs for the "counters." There should be three "counters" for every "issue" on the ballot (an election for office being an issue, in this case). So, for example, if there are twelve issues to be resolved, thirty six "counters" will be seated at the table. In previous preparation, thirty six small cards will have been prepared, with three cards designated for each ballot issue. These cards will be folded once, paper clipped, and placed in a small box which is then passed down the table for each counter to pick one. So, for example, a particular issue (for example, election for Mayor) will correspond to three cards randomly picked by three counters.

5. Once all counters are in place with their particular issues assigned, the ballot box may be opened and the first ballot retrieved. This ballot should be placed, face up, under a camera linked to the Internet and to local recording devices for a minimum of three seconds. The ballot is then forwarded to the first counter, who will tally the indicated vote for the particular issue assigned to him or her, and then pass the ballot on to the next counter in line. The next ballot will then be removed from the ballot box, placed under the camera for three seconds, and forwarded to the first counter, and so on in like manner until the ballot box is empty. In this way each issue will be counted by three randomly assigned counters. Once a ballot has been counted by each counter it should be dropped into a second, locked, ballot box at the end of the counting tables.

6. Once all ballots have been counted, a group of three "judges" can call for the tallies, by issue, and on camera. If the tallies for all three counters are in agreement, then those tallies are noted as the official result. If the tallies for two counters agree, but a third is discrepant by less than one percent, then the tallies for the two agreeing counters should be used as the official result. If the results from all three counters are discrepant, then the particular issue should be set aside for a recount, and the next issue queried. Once all issues have been queried, those issues that meet the requirement of at least two counters in agreement and the third less than one percent different may be judged to be official and complete. Those issues that do not meet this requirement and been set aside should be recounted. This can be accomplished by simply replacing all of the ballots in the ballot box, reassigning counters for the issues to be resolved, and repeating the procedure described in step **5**, above.

7. Eventually, all issues will have been successfully counted. The results of these counts may then be entered on an official "Statement of Results" and witnessed by signing by all witnesses, counters, and judges present. This statement of results, and the signatures thereon, should then be scanned and made available for direct download on the Internet, and directly placed under a camera and streamed to the Internet for the next twenty four hours. If a copy machine is available, copies of the "Statement of Results" can also be made for posting on the door and for any interested parties to take with them. The actual ballots should be placed in the hands of three trusted custodians for safe keeping.

ASSUMING A THOUSAND voters in a particular precinct, and five seconds for a counter to tally each vote, then it will take five thousand seconds to tally all of the ballots cast. Five thousand seconds is less than an hour and a half. Surely we can find a few hours to hand count our ballots transparently and *know* that they represent voter intent.

Once each precinct tally is available, it is a simple matter to accumulate overall totals. This could safely be done electronically because the original paper trail will be so abundantly transparent and available to any interested party, with records of the whole procedure stored everywhere anyone has in interest. The images of all precinct "Statement of Results" would be all that is needed to make a very convincing argument for the validity of a particular election issue anywhere it is needed. Compared to the face validity of the current electronic methods, which is clearly zero . . . there is simply no contest.

Chapter 8 — An Amendment Defining Political Bribery and the Punishment Therefore

JOINT RESOLUTION

Proposing an amendment to the Constitution defining Bribery of a Public Official of the United States and how such Bribery shall be punished.

Resolved by the Senate and House of Representatives of the United States of America in Congress assembled (two-thirds of each House concurring therein), That the following article is proposed as an amendment to the Constitution, which shall be valid to all intents and purposes as part of the Constitution when ratified by the legislatures of three-fourths of the several States.

ARTICLE _ _ _ _ _ _ _ _ _ _ _ _ _

"The right of citizens of the United States to honest representation shall not be denied or abridged

by the practice of political bribery of an elected official within the United States for any reason.

"Bribery is defined as anything given or serving to persuade or induce.

"All contributions supporting a political campaign are presumed to be bribes unless clearly proven otherwise.

"Political bribery is a betrayal of the citizens of the United States, and shall be punishable with a minimum of five years imprisonment for each count of bribery that causes no public harm, and life without parole, or death, for each count that causes demonstrable public harm.

"The crime of Bribery shall apply equally to individuals who offer bribes and those individuals who accept them.

"The value of all proceeds obtained through Bribery shall be trebled and made forfeit to the United States treasury.

(Signed)

Speaker of the House of Representatives.

(Signed)

Vice President of the United States and President of the Senate.

This amendment gets to the heart of the problems we face: bribery is the direct means by which exclusive political control of the government of We, the People is maintained by the wealthy. These bribes are currently legal, because they are *defined* as "campaign contributions." Never mind that they are intended or serve to "persuade or induce." I live in Florida, so let me use Florida statutes as an example to illustrate how this works.

The Florida statutes contain an entire chapter entitled: **"BRIBERY; MISUSE OF PUBLIC OFFICE."** (**FS 838**) which serves to provide convenient "cover" so that our public officials can point to it and loudly proclaim: "Hey, look at this! We have REALLY NASTY laws against all kinds of bribery." For example: **Florida Statute 838.015 Bribery** and **Florida Statute 838.016 Unlawful compensation or reward for official behavior**.

It sounds great, doesn't it? But the Big-Bucks Boys continue to openly give huge sacks of money to our politicians all the time, and just coincidentally these "donations" correlate very closely with favorable legislation or largess - - - so why isn't this bribery under the law? These politicians can't get elected without this money, so it seems unlikely that it is not influencing, and the definition of a Bribe is pretty straightforward: "Anything given or serving to persuade or induce[27]."

Ah, but there is a huge loophole in our Florida bribery laws. A loophole that would make Machiavelli proud, because it is hidden in plain sight and not often noticed. Florida has draconian laws against bribery, but under Florida law nobody can say with certainty exactly what bribery is. **Florida Statute 838.014 Definitions** clearly defines: "Benefit," "Bid," "Commodity," "Corruptly," "Harm," "Public servant," and "Service," but it does *not* contain

---

[27]Random House Dictionary of the English Language, 1968

any definition of a "bribe" or "bribery" *at all*; even though the entire Chapter 838 is presumably about this very issue. Was this an oversight, or done intentionally? This rather obvious omission leaves anything that can in any way be construed as "something else" as an open loophole through which our entire legislative body may collectively leap while holding hands and sanctimoniously pointing to "their draconian laws against bribery."

So, in Florida, you probably couldn't get away with meeting with your Representative and directly handing him a sack of money in return for a personal tax break written into the law just for you. That would definitely be illegal. But you most certainly *can* buy that tax break if you call your sack of money a campaign contribution. Then it's perfectly legal. Under Florida law, defining money as a "campaign contribution" effectively excludes that money from the definition of a "bribe" simply because there is no such definition! That tax break legislation you buy with your "campaign contribution" would therefore be passed "for the benefit of the citizens of the state," . . . of course.

THERE IS ANOTHER SIDE to the bribery equation worthy of note. In the early part of the last century Henry Ford got into trouble by trying to be a nice guy. He wanted to use corporate profits that he viewed as excessive to raise worker salaries and reduce the price of his company's automobiles. His stockholders objected, and took him to court.[28] They wanted that money for themselves, and they got it. The judge ruled that the whole purpose of

---

[28] Dodge v. Ford, 1919

business is to maximize shareholder wealth, and if Ford "wanted to pursue a [charitable end] he should do it with his own money, not with other people's."

The principle forged into law by Dodge v. Ford continues today to *force* corporate management to maximize stockholder profits. The law has been modified slightly since 1980 to allow for a slightly more "social" flavor, but the "fiduciary responsibility" of corporate management this principle established remains firmly in place. Since the Dodge v. Ford ruling, CEOs have been *required by law* to have a clear and "reasonable expectation of profit" when they spend stockholder money. Interestingly, the requirement for a "reasonable expectation of profit" applies to corporate political campaign contributions and "issue ads" just like any other expenditure. These facts bring up an interesting implication. When corporate money is given to a politician *the only possible return for this investment is favorable legislation.* Corporations that spend money for political purposes are openly engaged in political bribery, in other words, even if they call it something else like a "campaign contribution" or an "issue ad." But, since both our politicians and our plutocrats gain, and are in charge, this practice will never be legally challenged. Our wealthy are above the law, after all, and will not allow it. Moreover, *the corporate fiduciary duty to stockholders has been provably maintained. The profits from corporate political "expenditures" are phenomenal, and both our politicians and the plutocrats that control them have no incentive to change anything.* You might want to make a change, though, since their profits are your losses.

There is no easy way to estimate the specific return our corporations realize from political investments, but it must be tremendous because the investments themselves are quite high. In 2010 representatives serving in the House received $1,088,492,264 in "campaign contributions;" in the Senate $745,112,864; and President Obama (not running that year) received $18,106.[29]

To get some sense of the incredible magnitude of the return on these investments, consider just one issue. In 2010 a primary issue was health care reform. In that year, $142,074,788[30] was "contributed" by the health care industry to our politicians. Politicians have nothing but their legislation to offer in return for this money, and common sense tells us that promoting legislation that would reduce profits — really wasn't the idea. Indeed, any politician receiving a portion of the health care industry's $142 million giveaway could be expected to irritate his "benefactors" mightily if his legislation were to, say, actually reduce health care costs — and thus industry profits. Common sense also tells us that any congressman who reduced health care costs would be immediately "cut off" from his health care industry corporate largess, and would last about as long in his job "representing the people" as any faint hint of morality lasts in congress.

2010 was a very scary year for the health care industry. Any sensible congressman actually trying to reduce health care costs would clearly have opted for a single payer system, simply because it costs half as much and produces far superior results. This fact has been proven clearly, worldwide. If congress were to do this, however, the money thus saved by We, the People would be *profits not collected* by the health care industry. The health care industry's $142 million was clearly spent to prevent single payer from destroying those profits, and it worked. When you can spend a mere $142 million to gain monopolistic

---

[29]http://www.opensecrets.org/overview/index.php

[30]http://www.opensecrets.org/industries/totals
.php?cycle=2010&ind=H

control of a *multi-trillion* dollar cash cow . . . that's an extremely good return on investment!

But, alas, for some reason I remain exceedingly irritated at being sold out so cheaply. Senator Max Baucus was, for example, widely reported to have received at least $4 million of that health care industry investment. A payment which, with just over 306 million Americans in the country, works out to a little over a penny to betray each citizen. This was money that Senator Baucus "earned" for doing his part to legalize an effective monopoly that allows the health care industry to impose "your money or your life" extortion upon us all. A valuable monopoly that, when you factor in the price of all the other congressmen involved, cost the health care industry a grand total of roughly 46 cents for each of us, but which legalized the extortion of tens of thousands of dollars *from* each of us. Surely this monopoly was worth more than 46 cents!

Congress missed a perfect opportunity to have an auction. They could have asked We, the People to bid against the health care industry and probably increased their "take" by an order of magnitude or more! If Senator Baucus, for example, had given us the opportunity to make a direct payment to him for his support, we probably could have bought public health care with a one-time payment of less than fifteen cents from each of us to Max (less than $5 from each of us altogether) . . . and Max would have kicked that mere four million dollars in silver pieces up to almost forty six million!

Our current crop of politicians can't even do graft well. Constantly betraying We, the People must destroy brain cells. Or, maybe it's the drugs and alcohol they use to sleep at night that destroys those cells.

Chapter 9 — An Amendment Limiting the Size and Power of Business Entities

JOINT RESOLUTION

Proposing an amendment to the Constitution defining the method by which the people of the United States shall limit the size and power of business entities.

Resolved by the Senate and House of Representatives of the United States of America in Congress assembled (two-thirds of each House concurring therein), That the following article is proposed as an amendment to the Constitution, which shall be valid to all intents and purposes as part of the Constitution when ratified by the legislatures of three-fourths of the several States after a one year grace period to allow the affected entities to adjust as required.

ARTICLE _ _ _ _ _ _ _ _ _ _ _ _ _

"The right of citizens of the United States to freedom from predation by business entities that have become large enough to interfere with government functions shall be enforced by the United States.

"Any economic segment within the United States or its territories that is comprised of fewer than one hundred individual and independent business entities is potentially monopolistic.

"An economic segment within the meaning of this amendment is defined as a single entity or a multitude of separable entities producing the same or similar products that anticipate the same or similar end use or market.

"Business entities defined as potentially monopolistic will be subject to a 110% tax on all asset value and/or income exceeding one billion dollars. All other applicable taxes shall apply to any residual value remaining after the application of this tax.

"Business entities defined as potentially monopolistic shall apply a cap of 40 times the wage of the lowest paid worker within said economic entity to all workers, officers, and stockholders of said economic entity. If said cap is exceeded, a 110% tax shall be applied to the full gross value of said excess.

"Business entities defined as potentially monopolistic shall be limited to the production and sale of a single product type. Product types shall be defined as items that would be naturally classified together for sale to an end user. For example, *soap, automobiles, hand tools, and computers would all be separate product classifications.*

"In all cases where a single business entity manufactures multiple products for sale in multiple markets, the total value of all sales from all markets for that entity shall be used when determining if any of those products is potentially monopolistic.

(Signed)

Speaker of the House of Representatives.

(Signed)

Vice President of the United States and President of the Senate.

A MAJOR ABSURDITY within the United States is the existence of business entities that are deemed "*Too Large to Fail*" by our government. Any sensible government actually working for the good of the country would consider these entities very differently: as *Too Large to Allow to Exist*, and break them up! Any business entity large enough to influence government, or endanger the overall economy, is simply too dangerous to allow continued existence. This fact is obvious — unless you happen to be on their payroll. Business entities are driven by a predatory nature, and in a competitive environment this is a good thing since most of this drive is channeled into competitive activities that benefit society as a whole. When this drive becomes unfettered, as it always will when every horizon has already been conquered and all or nearly all competitors consumed or destroyed, we are left with oligopolistic systems that are detrimental to everyone, including the owners of those companies. The people suffer, because prices are artificially raised. The business entities themselves suffer, because without competition to keep them on their toes and sharp they will decline and die a bloated natural death as new technologies render them obsolete in spite of their every effort to remain in the past.

The United States economy did fairly well after World War II, up until the early seventies. We had strong antitrust laws, and regulations that limited the predation of our business entities. In spite of these laws and regulations, however, by the seventies our largest business entities had concentrated their power to the point that our government was completely controlled by them via political bribery of one sort or another. The death knell for our economy occurred when Ronald Reagan stopped enforcing antitrust laws in the eighties. The result of Reagan's action was acquisition following merger until now there are no competitive markets in the United States at all. All major industries and markets are dominated by oligopolistic members; usually three to ten in number, because that is sufficient to claim they are not "really" monopolistic while at the same time leaving monopolistic behavior completely unfettered.

Oligopolies always behave very much like monopolies. All the members of oligopolies are smart enough to realize that competing with the other members is not to their advantage. No secret meetings are needed to cement this unspoken agreement, just a healthy self interest. So, price competition simply doesn't happen within an oligopolistic industry. As a result, all their customers pay excessively high prices for their products.

ECONOMIES OF SCALE[31] are another very important reason to break up our business entities. Economies of scale refer to the fact that in almost any production situation the unit cost of production drops, then rises, as a function of production volume. That is, production unit cost plotted as a function of production volume will produce a "U" shaped curve. Ideally, production should be limited to the volume corresponding to the bottom of the "U." This is where both the greatest profit per unit is found, and the lowest possible price per unit is found . . . if the advantage of this position is passed on to the consumer.

In a truly competitive industry various factors such as price and production costs will tend to work together to put a product on the market at the best possible price. This is because increasing volume that increases to the point where the cost per unit is increasing becomes self limiting as competitors stay in the most efficient part of the curve and can keep their prices lower. On the left side of the curve, however, as increasing production decreases costs, the entity doing this can afford to lower their asking price, which results in more production, and moves that entity closer to the rising portion of the cost curve. In this case real market behavior can be exactly as classical theory would predict . . . but only if there are sufficient production entities to have actual competition. A hundred or more is probably enough because someone in that group will be greedy enough to try to undercut the others. Three to ten entities, our current oligopolies in other words, are few enough for "silent understandings" to the detriment of all.

THIS AMENDMENT SEEKS to limit the size of busi-

---

[31]http://en.wikipedia.org/wiki/Economies_of_scale

ness entities that, for whatever reason, become members of oligopolistic industries. Business entities are allowed to grow unfettered in any way they wish up to a capitalization of one billion dollars. This size is large enough to establish the tooling to produce any product efficiently, but small enough to prevent their interference with others who might want to compete. If some larger product production is required there is nothing in the amendment that would prevent separate entities working together, say, by making different parts to be sold to a third entity. A third entity could then do final assembly, for example, and sell the final product. But entities which grow to the point where they are hogging enough of the market to get the number of their competitors below one hundred separate entities will trigger the definition of "potentially monopolistic" and get restrictions slapped on them that the owners will not like. These restrictions are intended as a brake on expansion that makes it desirable to keep things modest and to not use predatory tactics to destroy competition. This amendment should really make our current CEO's scream. It will cut into their personal largess considerably, because they will have to compete for a change. This is a good thing.

Chapter 10 — A Few Final Words

Out of this modern civilization economic royalists [have] carved new dynasties....It was natural and perhaps human that the privileged princes of these new economic dynasties, thirsting for power, reached out for control over government itself. They created a new despotism and wrapped it in the robes of legal sanction....And as a result the average man once more confronts the problem that faced the Minute Man.

These economic royalists complain that we seek to overthrow the institutions of America. What they really complain of is that we seek to take away their power.

And our allegiance to American institutions requires the overthrow of this kind of power!

Franklin D. Roosevelt, 1936

John F. Kennedy famously stated that ***Those who make peaceful revolution impossible will make violent revolution inevitable.*** This statement has worried me greatly for years, as I fear he is correct and that violent revolution is all but upon us now. The level of anger in the United States that is directed at our government and the wealthy elites that control it is palpable. The government, in their turn, is so confident of their ability to maintain their power that they no longer bother to disguise their nefarious behavior. These thoughts were instrumental to my thinking when I wrote "*Sedition Awakening*," a novel about as bloodless a violent revolution as I could imagine. But there is another thought that scares me more, a thought put into print over two hundred years ago by Edmund Burke that, if put into practice at this time, will make violent revolution absolutely inevitable, just as President Kennedy so eloquently states. That disquieting thought is simply this:

> ***All that is necessary for the triumph of evil is that good men do nothing.***

> ***Edmund Burke (January 12, 1729 – July 9, 1797)***

For years I have helplessly watched as my fellow citizens persistently do nothing in the face of obvious evil. Where is their civic virtue? Where is their sense of honor? As pointed out in Chapter two, Edward Gibbon argues in his *Fall of the Roman Empire* that Roman citizens allowed the decline of their empire because they lacked civic virtue. Gibbon felt that this lack of civic virtue was brought about by the Roman adoption of Christianity, and its implied premise that a reward in heaven for "good" behavior (obeying authority) removed them from the responsibility of living in the here and now; which is, according to Christian doctrine, God's responsibility. Or, perhaps the lack of civic virtue in the United States is simply because We, the People have been conditioned since birth to obey authorities, and carefully taught to think of ourselves as helpless. Or, most disquieting, perhaps the mass of our population is simply so selfish and so conditioned to think of "consumption" as their entire purpose in life that they cannot think beyond their own immediate hedonistic gratification, and are, in my view if this is true, not worth the trouble to save from themselves.

I have good reason to fear Mr. Burke's warning. Several years ago I attempted to get the amendment described in Chapter eight (Bribery) onto the Florida ballot via a citizen referendum. I set up a web site with an integrated blog as an information center for this effort called BreakTheLink.org; registered the effort with the Florida state government, and spent two years begging and pleading for people to help. There were hundreds of posts on the blog, with almost all being positive and encouraging. But with over fifteen thousand people who visited and apparently read the site, there was extremely little actual participation in the effort. A close friend helped me gather a hundred or so of the signatures required, and another person helped with the official paperwork. When my friend and I were in the park to gather signatures, just about everyone we asked signed. Who isn't against political bribery, after all? But it would seem that a lot of people will talk the talk, but walking the walk is just too much to ask. After a couple of years of trying, I gave it up and shut down the site . . . and Mr. Burke's comment haunts me still.

I like to think that this time will be different. The recent protests in Wisconsin are encouraging. Our politicians seem intent on ruining our economy and our government so the wealthy can use us all as serfs, and they aren't even bothering to try and hide their agenda. The fact that they no longer bother to hide their agenda is a clear warning that they think they have things so under control that they don't need to. If we do not find the means to turn their project around, they will clearly succeed. It will be more of "their way, or the highway," with the highway option meaning homelessness or work camps, and starving.

The greedy parasites that run our country only follow their nature, and that nature is to acquire. This process would be far more benign if there were fewer of them, but with the several hundred individuals now attempting to take control of absolutely everything, nobody is left with any power to intelligently run the country, or the world. Perhaps the acquisitory class simply can't think that far ahead. Or, perhaps the wealthy are determined to render us helpless because they, at least, *can* see the dire future we face with increasing population, peak oil, climate change and the very real prospect of wide spread anarchy. They must think that when they have *all* the money, and thus complete control, that their money will protect them. They forget that money isn't intrinsically useful, and is just paper when not supported by a viable social system. The same is almost as true of precious metals and the like. A good stock of stainless steel is far more intrinsically useful than a huge stock of gold.

Perhaps you feel the urgency of getting our government governing instead of facilitating theft as strongly as I do. I certainly hope so. The wealthy want to sooth you with lies about how we have at least a century to work on the climate issue, and to assure you that all our weapons will keep us safe . . . and so on. Do you believe it? I don't. I am a trained scientist with an engineering background.

I know an exponential phenomenon when I see one, and that is exactly what we are within on the climate issue. Consider a small experiment in non-linear phenomena to illustrate the problem. Push on a toggle type switch lever (a wall light switch, for example) as slowly as you can, and see what happens. Initially it will move just as slowly as you push it, then suddenly, without any warning, it will accelerate in the same direction you were pushing faster than the blink of an eye. That is what our climate is about to do when the sea water warms to the melting point of ice at the poles, a phenomenon which has already started. Way before the melting ice raises sea levels enough to be a serious problem, methane gas now sequestered in ice on the sea bed will be released in massive quantities and spike global warming into an ever accelerating positive feedback loop. Just like that wall switch, if you don't push too far you can back off. But at some point it will simply be too late and the process will run to completion, no matter what we do. Snap!

Initially, if we are foolish enough to continue on our present path, new weather patterns will cause crops to fail and hungry people will be out trying to steal food, no doubt with weapons. Never once in our history have humans just quietly sat down and died for the convenience of their neighbors. It's just not in our nature. Exacerbating this issue is the fact that our delicately intertwined systems are inherently fragile. Anyone who has lived through a hurricane, as I have, knows how little it takes to bring the whole system of food and fuel distribution to a halt. Hurricanes are local in their effect, and outside aid is usually forthcoming to mitigate most of the effects. When the disruption is national, or world wide, things will be very different. It will take very little actual disruption to *snap* our now viable but intricately intertwined support systems over to . . . nonviable.

THE POINT I am trying to make is simply this: if *you* persist in doing nothing, persist in leaving the job to "somebody else," ignore your civic responsibilities and enough of your fellow citizens do the same, your survival is unlikely, and your children's survival is a non-issue: they definitely won't. The situation we now face is unprecedented in human history, and exactly that serious. It is not unprecedented in planetary history, however. There have been at least five major mass extinctions so far, three of which followed essentially the same path we are now on. On those occasions it was an increase in volcanic activity that released the CO_2 into the atmosphere and initiated the process, now it's us.

In a direct competition for survival with the cockroach family *our* species has little chance if this trend runs to completion. In fact, given our propensity for violence before reasoned action, humans probably have less chance of survival right now than just about *any* other major species, at least initially. That gloomy prediction is made without taking into account the fact that our demise will no doubt completely foul the planet for most other species as well.

THE PLAN PRESENTED in this Handbook is a long-shot, but at least it's a plan. It takes advantage of the near universal perspective in the United States that we are a democracy, and have the right to vote, neither of which are currently true if accurate vote *counting* is included. If you just attempt to demonstrate these points to the public, you will cast a seed of doubt in a few minds. If you and a few others demonstrate clearly how a transparent election can be done, those seeds of doubt will grow, and sprout with the corollary knowledge of how nontransparent our "official" election procedures have become. This increased awareness has no other interpretation than this: our government is *preventing* democracy, both representative and otherwise. This realization will breed anger, and anger can be turned into collective action that reestablishes our representative democracy.

The impact this program will have on the public mind is directly related to your ability to present a completely transparent and honest means of holding elections. There must be no place in the system that is remotely questionable. No place for our enemies to insert doubt, as they most assuredly will try. Everything must be open, available for examination, and verifiable. Not a secret in sight, and no possibility of one. If you can do this, then the very *honorableness* of the endeavor will win the hearts of We, the People and move them to help you.

Honest elections, once achieved, provide the means of obtaining further reform. Winning the honest elections battle will form the basis for an enhanced public *confidence*. A "we *can* fight 'city hall,' and *win*" confidence which can then be directed toward actual government changes such as the amendments in chapters seven, eight, and nine.

IN CLOSING, LET me point out that this is a very old fight. Harriet Beecher Stowe wrote the words below in 1863, in reference to our Civil War. They could have been written yesterday. Her words demonstrate clearly that it is well past the time to get organized and make the effort and the sacrifices necessary to win this battle decisively. I strongly suspect that we are down to less than a decade to turn things around, and that only if we start now.

*The revolution through which the
American nation is passing is not a*

mere local convulsion. It is a war for principle, which concerns all mankind. It is the war for the working classes of mankind as against the usurpations of privileged aristocracies. You can make nothing else out of it. That is the reason why, like a shaft of light in the Judgment Day, it has gone through all nations – dividing to the right and left the multitudes. For us and our cause: all the common working classes of Europe, all that toil and sweat and are oppressed. Against us: all privileged classes, nobles, princes, bankers, and great manufacturers, and all who live at ease. A silent instinct piercing to the dividing of soul and spirit, joints and marrow, has gone through the earth, and sent every soul with instinctive certainty where it belongs. No sophistry could blind or deceive them. They knew that our cause was their cause, and they have suffered their part heroically as if fighting by our side, because they knew that our victory was to be their victory. On the other side, all aristocrats and holders of exclusive privileges have felt the instinctive opposition, and the sympathy with struggling aristocracy, for they too feel that our victory will be their doom.

William Bradford Cushman